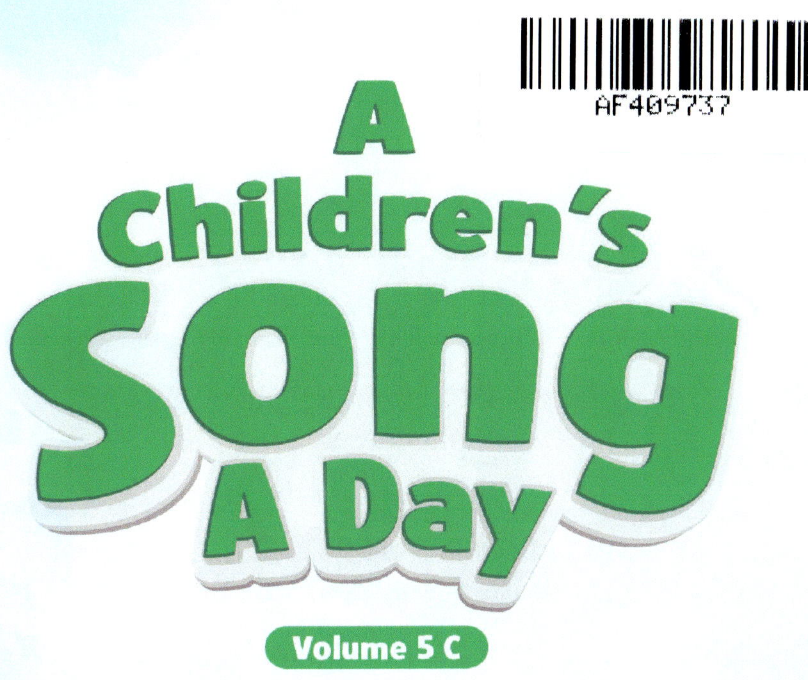

Dr. Swapna Abraham

ISBN
Paperback 979-8-89415-291-2
Hardcase 979-8-89475-644-8

DEDICATION

Dedicated to my children and grandchildren
And written for the children (and adults) of the world

GOLDEN BOOK OF WORLD RECORDS

GOLDEN
BOOK OF WORLD RECORDS
TM

Certificate of Excellence

LONGEST QUOTIDIAN FEAT OF COMPOSING, PRODUCING AND PUBLISHING CHILDREN'S SONG INCESSANTLY

The World Record of "longest quotidian feat of composing, producing and publishing children's song incessantly" has been achieved by Swapna Abraham from Dubai, United Arab Emirates.

During Apr 08, 2017 - Jan 02, 2020; Swapna has live composed, produced and published a children's song incessantly for One Thousand (1000) days.

Golden Book of World Records

This certificate must not be reproduced without the permission of Golden Book of World Records.
www.goldenbookofworldrecords.com

INSTRUCTIONS & INFORMATION

- The QR code with the logo is of the song and the QR code without the logo is of the karaoke/ sing-along called minus. Should any of the codes get damaged with use, please mail the author at music@swapnaabraham.com for a copy of the code specifying song number and title.
- The songs and karaokes can be played scanning the QR code with the scanner on a mobile phone or tablet.
- A Children's Song A Day is a collection of 1000 children's songs compiled in five volumes.
- The 'live' composing of the songs on A Children's Song A Day are chronicled on https://www.facebook.com/achildrenssongaday. In addition to this song, everyday, through the 1000 days, the author composed another regular song (https://www.facebook.com/swapnaabraham1000songsin1000days). Hailing from a gospel music background, for 100 of the 1000 days, the author composed yet another exclusive gospel song everyday (https://www.facebook.com/profile.php?id=100057060476408); and for 40 of the 1000 days, the author collated lyrics from the Book of Psalms and composed five additional songs everyday (https://www.facebook.com/profile.php?id=100063496163428). Lastly on the 999th day, the author composed an additional 20 songs (https://www.facebook.com/profile.php?id=100063886660578).

The whole effort through the 1000 days set four world records with the Golden Book of World Records:

- Longest quotidian feat of composing, producing and publishing song incessantly (April 08, 2017 - January 02, 2020)
- Quotidian feat of composing, producing and publishing multiple songs incessantly for 100 days (March 08, 2019 - June 15, 2019)
- Most songs composed, produced and published by an individual in one day (January 01, 2020)
- Longest quotidian feat of composing, producing and publishing children's song incessantly [they do not consider the children's song as a regular song, but certainly call it children's song] (April 08, 2017 - January 02, 2020)
  For more details: https://www.1000songsin1000days.com/

The author published a book 'She Played In The Dark' (available on Amazon and Kindle) entailing the journey and lessons through the 1000 days with references from her past.

- Should a child or just about anyone record a video of any of the songs on A Children's Song A Day, do remember to tag https://www.instagram.com/a_childrens_song_a_day/, https://www.youtube.com/channel/UCjOcB3bgn39hD8NmCCBcp0Q, or/ and https://www.facebook.com/achildrenssongaday in your post.
- The author would love to hear your experiences with A Children's Song A Day at music@swapnaabraham.com.

DISCLAIMER

All the songs on A Children's Song A Day were composed with no use of AI.

Contents

SONG TO GOD

I lift my hands up in praise
My voice in song I'll raise
To thank you
For all of my days

I rejoice in your presence
A pure heart like incense
At all times
You are my defence

Hallelujah *2
Hala hala Hallelujah
Hallelujah *2

SO LITTLE

They are so little
Hearts and limbs small
Yes, they are little
One day they'll be tall
You see them little
Some day they'll be all
Let the children live *2

COUGH AWAY

Cough away *3
You'll be better some day
Cough away *3
The trouble will not stay

Stay away from cold and hay
Stay away ok

DONATE

WHY CAN'T WE

With just a little caring
And a little sharing
We can feed them all
The earth has enough
For all the weak and tough
So we can feed them all

Why can't we

ALL THE WAY UP

All the way up
No looking down
Keep going up
Never looking down

Step by step
Breath by breath
Mile by mile
You will reach the top
And I'll see you smile

HERE WE ARE

Here we are *2
Writing songs
To sing along

Music and lyric
Heart and soul
That's all we need
Magic and comic
More heart and soul
That's all we need

BUBBLE MAGIC

Bubbles in the bath
Troubles flowing path
Bubbles in the bath
Just like magic

Bubbles in the air
Water circles everywhere
Bubbles in the air
Feels like magic, magic to me

IN THE MORNING

When we rise in the morning
We thank the Lord for the day
With praise
For good and warning
We thank the Lord and pray
Hands raised

Surrender everything in his hands
Those big hands
Surrender everything in his love

THIS STAR

I play my guitar
Just like a star
I'm heard from near and far
It's more than a dream
Makes my father beam
One day I'll have a team

POP
ROCK

SING WITH ME

Sing with me *2
Truly
Let's sing and be merry
Sing with me *2
Coolly
All legendary

Sing with me *2
Freely
Let's sing and be merry
Sing with me *2
Really
All legendary

THE DIVINE MERCY CHAPLET FOR CHILDREN

Eternal father
I offer you the body and blood
Soul and divinity of your dearly beloved son
Our Lord Jesus Christ

In atonement
For our sins
And those of the whole world

For the sake of his sorrowful passion
Have mercy on us and on the whole world

Holy God
Holy mighty one
Holy immortal one
Have mercy on us and on the whole world

PS: The prayer of St. Faustina Kowalska

SPECIAL ONE

I know she misses me
And I miss her too
I know she wishes
Just the best and true

Waiting to see her
All the fun with her
My special one just for me

CLAP
CLAP

MY TWO SMALL ALL

With my two small hands

I can clap

My two small feet

I can jump

My two small ears and eyes

I can hear and see

With my two small hands

I can flap

My two small feet

I can thump

My two small ears and eyes

I perceive

PIRATE

TO THE PLAYGROUND

We go round and round
Round and round
On the merry-go-round

We go up and down
Up and down
On the swing and slide

We go back and forth
Back and forth
To the playground

HIDE AND SEEK

You will never find me *3
When I'm hiding

Until you find me *3
That's hide and seek

TIME WITH FAMILY

Family *2
Spend more time with family
Family *2
Spend more time at home

There's a time for friends
There's a time for school
There's a time for everyone
But more for family

PLANTS AND WE

All it needs is a good seed
Good soil and a good deed
Sunlight, water and minerals
What we give out, they take in
Air we breathe together
Plants and we

DON'T FORGET TO REST

Work and chores
Keep you busy all day
More work and chores
And a little play
Work and chores
Keep an idle mind away
But don't forget to rest

GOD'S FAVOURITE

I am God's favourite
And so are you
He's given me so much
As he's given you too
If only we knew the perfect fit
Of God's favourite

THIS RAINBOW

I'll fly on top of the rainbow
I'll try to cross the seven bows
Such wonder how it comes and goes
This rainbow

WAIT

When somebody's talking
Wait
When somebody's trying
Wait

When you cross the road
Lift a load
When you're in a queue
Or in the pew

LIVE IT UP

Today is the first day
Of the rest of your life
Live it up *2
Today is the first day
Of the rest of our lives
Live it up, let's live it up

Come what may
Good or bad
Let's live it up

DO IT AGAIN

When you do it again
Do it again and again
Do it again
You'll be the best you can

And be the best you can
Be the best you can
Be the best there is, the best you can

A SECRET

When you're told a secret
Keep the secret
Don't share the secret with anyone
When you're told a secret
Hold the secret
Don't show the secret for fun

WHEN I'M ANGRY

What should I do
When I'm feeling angry
What should I do
When I'm blue
What should I do
When I'm so angry
Count to twenty-two

So angry *3
Me

PRAISE

Praise *2 him
Praise him when we're sad
Praise *2 him
Praise him when we're glad

Alleluia, alleluia *2

WORRIES

You don't worry at all
Don't worry at all
Pick all your worries and send them away
Don't worry at all *2
Drop all your worries today

We don't worry at all
Don't worry at all
Pick all our worries and send them away
Don't worry at all *2
Drop all our worries today

START AND END

Everything must have an end
Remember this when you send
Everything comes to a close
Think of this, who knows

Someone show me the start
Someone show me the end
Someone show me the art
I cannot pretend

STAY WITH ME

Stay with me *2
Everyday, please stay
Stay with me *2
All the way, please stay

I'm all on my own
So alone

Stay with me *2
Everyday, please stay

6
4
3
5
2

GET OUTSIDE AND PLAY

Hop, skip and jump *3
Around the stump
Go up and down *3
Play the clown

Get outside and play
Run around the bay
A real getaway
Everyday

YOUR PARENTS

Listen to them *2
Love and obey your parents
Listen to them *2
Love and obey them

You are with them
They are with you
You're with each other
Stuck like glue

IT COMES AROUND

What goes around
Comes around
Up and down
It comes around
Round about
It comes around
Left and right to you

THE BEST

Oh ho ho! You're beautiful
Gentle, true and kind
Oh ho ho! You're wonderful
The best I'll ever find

You're the best I'll ever find

SAILING

I'm sailing in my boat
Across the silver lake
My little paddle boat
A little give and take

Slowly we row (oh oh oh)
Slowly we go (oh oh oh)
Slowly we cross the silver lake

MAN WITH THE BEARD

I saw a man with a long beard
How they feared
Oh! The man with a long beard
All men feared

And everywhere he went
They would stare at him
Everywhere he went
The beard would go with him

LOVE

Love is such a miracle
Love change the debacle
Love is on a pinnacle
Love makes the world go

Round and round a miracle
Changing every debacle
Standing on a pinnacle
Love makes the world go (round)

GIVING

I've been given a lot
To give some to you
I've been given a lot
But some was meant for you

To give some to you *3
And that's what I'll do

PURPLE HEART

A purple heart
Is a soldier's heart
A brave heart
And a strong heart
A purple heart
A happy purple heart

I LET HIM IN

He was standing at the door and knocking
I opened and let him in
It was a mystery
He set me free
And we had a cup of tea

He's making me happy
So happy
Showed me right from wrong
Hold on to him and I'll be strong

TO SAVE THE WORLD

All the children of the world
Come together
To save the world

Love and hope and cleaner air
Save the world

Food for all, clothes and toys
Save the world

Fun and games and smiling faces
Save the world

MAKE A WISH

Make a wish upon a star
Make a wish when you see it from afar
Make a wish on your guitar
Make a wish when you feel it
Wish when you hear it
Wish upon a star

ORDER

Papa papapa papapapa
Papa papapapapa
Tadadada
Papa papapa papapapa
Papapa

Who's first goes first
Who's last goes last
Bad to worst
And now to past

Forward

1 2 3 4 5 6 7 8

Backward

8 7 6 5 4 3 2 1

COUNTING

1 2 3 4 5 6 7 8

Counting forward now

8 7 6 5 4 3 2 1

Counting backward now

SOMETHING IN EVERYTHING

There's something in everything
In everything you had
Something in everything
The good and the bad
There's something if you see it
And nothing if you don't
Something that will make you glad

DOWN THE MOUNTAIN

We should go down the mountain
When it's time
Go down the mountain
Past the climb
As beautiful as it could be
Magical to see
We should go down the mountain
When it's time

SAND AND MUD

It's a great thing
To play in the sand
Wish they could understand
It's a great thing to play in the sand
All day long

It's a great thing
To play in the mud
Wish they could hear the thud
It's a great thing to play in the mud
All day long

PITTER PATTER

Pitter patter
Sound of raindrops
No small matter
See how all stops

All the puddles
Become rivers
Lots of cuddles
Little shivers
All a muddle
Feel the quivers
When it rains
Pitter patter

THINGS I LOVE

I love red balloons
Silver bells and snowflakes
I love cartoons
Golden gel and cupcakes

I love you
I love all of you so much

JUST ONE

You're just one in a million
There are many other children
You're just one in a billion
Too many there like you

We're just one in a million
There are many other children
We're just one in a billion
Too many there like us

WINTER IS HERE

As I was walking down the street
I saw a snowflake, what a pretty sight
A sheet of white
Can feel a chill go up my spine
All I can say is it is time
Winter is here *2